GLASS HEARTS
& UNSPOKEN GOODBYES
Poems of HEALING AND hope

♥

Kayla McCullough

Andrews McMeel
PUBLISHING®

also by Kayla McCullough
Glass Hearts & Broken Promises

Andrews McMeel Publishing
a division of Andrews McMeel Universal
1130 Walnut Street, Kansas City, Missouri 64106

www.andrewsmcmeel.com

24 25 26 27 28 TEN 10 9 8 7 6 5 4 3 2 1

ISBN: 978-1-5248-9026-1

Library of Congress Control Number: 2023951817

Editor: Danys Mares
Art Director/Designer: Diane Marsh
Production Editor: Brianna Westervelt
Production Manager: Shona Burns

ATTENTION: SCHOOLS AND BUSINESSES
Andrews McMeel books are available at quantity discounts with
bulk purchase for educational, business, or sales promotional
use. For information, please e-mail the Andrews McMeel
Publishing Special Sales Department: sales@amuniversal.com.

dedication

for those who are needing to find
the beauty and joy in saying goodbye

contents

dear reader,

please remember
to hold on a little longer
remember to give
everything a fighting chance
remember to be patient
and when you're at your lowest
remember you're not alone

all my love,
Kayla

before we begin
I'd like to remind you that
the most beautiful part about you
is that you can heal
you can let go
and find your own way back home
to you again
because
you are strong
you are resilient
and it'll take more
than what made you feel worthless
to break you

◇ THE ◇
storm

I don't let many people in. I fear that the people I value
will someday move on with my heart still in their pockets.
I struggle to trust others and myself. But you, you were
different. You were a connection that my heart couldn't
resist. Something I never saw coming. A gift of spiritual
familiarity. A hand that I could reach for when everything
fell apart. My home in another body.

I don't think I'll ever be able to love
like this again, nor do I want to

I met you and overnight my world expanded
from me and my desires
to an endless realm
of love and possibility

you are the last person I ever want to love

I want to live in a world
where your love is all I know
where sunsets touch
every inch of my heart
and butterflies flutter
at the sound of your name

I want to hold on to this feeling
you, my love, are my everything

I want you
I want all of you
always and completely
I want your broken pieces
your scars and your bruises
I want to laugh with you
and I want to cry with you
I want to know your fears
and what excites you
I want to be there for you
to help you feel safe and heard
I want to grow with you
and share my life with you
the good, the bad, and the ugly
loving all of you comes naturally
and choosing you is a choice
that I will make every day

I would be lying if I said
that it was love at first sight
but I'd also be lying if I said
that my heart wasn't moved
the first time I saw you
somewhere deep down
I knew that it would be you
until the end

it's not like this with other people
you are not hard to love
I don't feel like I'm wasting time
when I'm with you
loving you is the easiest thing
I've ever done
but when you asked me again today
how much I loved you
I asked myself
how I could even answer that,
how do I describe this feeling?
because I'm so in love with you
that the thought of life without you
makes me lifeless

I pause and say
I love you so much that
I will love you until the world ends
and even still after that

Kayla McCullough

I feel like I am finally at home
when I am with you
I'm not alone anymore
the world no longer belongs
to just me and my mind
you hold my soul in your arms
and treat it like gold
you're a warm hug, a soft kiss,
and a kind smile
on days I feel lost and undeserving
your love is never-ending
I look back and watch
as temporary people leave
and I'm reminded that
even when momentary romance fades
you stand still in your place
with unchanging tenderness and
unwavering support
you are everything
I never knew I needed

I promise you

I will stay when it gets hard
I will stay when everyone else leaves
I will stay when the world is dark

I will stay

I promise you

my love for you
will never leave

It's because you're here when no one else is. You show up. You hold me and kiss my forehead and whisper all the reasons why you love me. I've never had to beg or silently plead to God that you'd be by my side when I needed you—you've always been there. Even on the days when I give you every reason under the sun not to show up, you do.

I finally believe in fate
in a world full of heartbeats
yours will always be the one
that will tear down my walls
and stare into the depths
of all my heart has known
all the damage
all the wounds
all the dark
and love me despite it

There is so much history in the way I feel about you. It's like I've known you for years. Every day feels less like I'm getting to know you and more like I'm remembering who you are. Every touch feels like something I've felt before. Every whisper sounds like vows I've promised before. There's so much familiarity between our hearts that every single thing makes me believe that I've loved you before.

the way you look at me
when you don't think I'm watching

feels like you love me
without you actually saying it

I want to wake up each morning knowing that even if the world crashes down on me, I will still have you.

I will still have you, and to me, that is always enough.

I will always remember the first time we met
my heart was racing out of my chest
the world started spinning
words barely formed
but somehow, I knew that I was yours

that night you followed me
into my dreams
and left me
waking up the next morning
craving your lips
I lost time imagining
what they tasted like
it was intoxicating

months passed and the world still spun
until the day you reached out
for my hand and kissed me
that's when I knew
I wanted to spend my entire life
with you

I once begged the universe for a love that would love everything about me. There would be no pretending, no shying away from the skeletons in our closets, no doubting the love we felt. We'd know each other's scars and never try to fix the broken parts. We'd just love each other for all that we were. That's what real love is—acceptance.

Somewhere in the universe there's another me meeting another you. It starts with a glance. I think that's how we begin in most stories. One look, one kiss, one touch of a hand, and suddenly our auras collide, and we know each other very well. A feeling of certainty washes over us and there's no turning back.

I loved you in a glance. In a handful of moments. I think you were always meant to hold me a little tighter than anyone else. I think in every universe we were always destined to be the culmination of a series of chain reactions and chance accidents that eventually find each other. I think in every universe we are one look, one kiss, one touch of a hand before we suddenly don't belong to ourselves anymore.

I'm sorry
for the people who did you wrong
the ones who you genuinely valued
with every fiber of your being
the ones you struggle
to let go of
for the people who had no remorse
who mishandled and mistreated
the magnitude of your love
I'm sorry

you deserve an apology
for the things that
nobody has apologized for

our love isn't perfect
but it's beautiful

it's real

If there were five million universes, I'd marry you in all except one. The last one? Perhaps that life belongs to a girl where time doesn't exist. She chases her way through Paris, walking in and out of stores, finding dreams left behind by strangers. She probably lives alone in a cottage the size of a shoebox, overlooking the water, and has tons of books littering the walls and floors. It's quiet here. No kids, but a dog she treats as her own. No friends, no flings, but a man who visits in her dreams. He's got dark hair with blue-green eyes and a soul that feels like she's known it for years. She never wants to wake up. The sunrise on anything that feels this magical in the dark is a scary thing; it loses something. But when the sleep wears off, and the feel of his touch disappears from her skin, when the endless possibilities slip away into the monotonous routine of moments spent beneath a cloudy Paris sky, nothing really feels the same. The world is louder somehow.

Sometimes, she lets these moments merge, the small ones, the ones when he touches the spot above her lips and flicks her hair out of her eyes and kisses her forehead. She scoops them up, collects them together in her mind, and thinks about the way that some moments purely exist for you to escape to. That's where she is most days, there in those dreams, asking herself if she'll ever find you.

no matter where I am
or who I'm with
a life with you
is what I want to live

we all want a love
without heartache
without pain or suffering
but that's a love
not worth remembering

so, embrace the struggles
and heartbreaks
because in the end
that's a love worth fighting for

Kayla McCullough

I fell in love on our third night, the first time I memorized
you completely, the last week before you flew back
home. I think of it still. Some nights, I thumb through our
story like pages of a well-loved book, pausing here and
there to read over my most cherished passages. I smile
at the pages of us learning each other. The unmade
beds and rumpled sheets. The patterns of our entangled
bodies burned into them permanently like a bloom of
light on a photograph. I skip to the end and think of all
the tears and hardships, every impossible odd against us,
until at last, I find myself right back at the very beginning,
sitting face-to-face with you in your car, suspended in a
breathless kiss.

love is a journey, not a destination
it takes you everywhere
from wonderstruck haze
to rock bottom
from hope-filled days
to anxiety-ridden nights
it's an everlasting constant
that grows and changes
it's the very thing that causes
your heart to ache
but the same thing
that makes it beat
love is the one thing
that will always prevail

I can tell you one thing. If your relationship feels as though it is crumbling beneath your very feet, you must both decide to strengthen it. Through actions and words and keeping your promises. Every day you must remind each other that this relationship is something very important to both of you. You might have five reasons why you should let this relationship go, but if there's even two or three reasons to save it, then you both must put in effort to make it stronger. All you have to ask yourself is, *Is this person worth the effort?* If your answer is yes, then you must put in the work.

I grew up in a divorced family and often struggle with the fear of abandonment. *What if you leave someday?* is a question that's made a home in my heart. It's why I try so hard in every relationship to fix what is broken, to love until it hurts. I overcompensate so that they never leave. But what I've learned is that you will never be able to stop those who want to leave. No matter how hard you try, no matter how many reasons you give them, they will always let you go. But I've also learned that those who want to stay will stay for only one reason and that is because of who you are.

It seems as though I may not meet you in this lifetime, but trust me, I will find you in the next.

~my soulmate

A Letter to Past Me

You fell in love this last year, and it wasn't pretty. You found out the hard way that fairy-tale romance doesn't last long. No matter how hard you try, it's destined to end with your heart in pieces. I know he's the center of your world right now, and it may feel like the two of you meeting was fate, but trust me, when you wake up on Tuesday, your heart will sink faster than the *Titanic*.

I wish time was kinder to you. There were so many signs you should have taken more seriously, so many people you should have believed. Which is why I'm here now, writing to you, hoping that someday past me will trust her intuition a little bit more. Maybe this letter somehow alters the future so that grief never becomes friends with someone so young. But I'm not that lucky. Even now, years later, I still struggle with learning when to let people go.

I digress. I'm going to have to break some bad news to you. Last night your dad passed away. Nothing and nobody will know how your heart will ache besides your sisters. Tell them, even though you may feel like you need to keep it all together. Tell them you love them. Tell them it hurts when you remember how your last conversation went. Tell them it feels like you've been betrayed, like somebody has punched you in the stomach. Tell them how sometimes it doesn't feel like anything at all. Because you are going to spend a lot of time wondering which feeling is worse. And I hope we can figure that out together one day.

When you go back to school after the funeral, don't go back to him. You're going to regret it. He'll never change, no matter what comes out of his mouth. I know all you want is to be loved. You want it so bad you'll betray yourself for it. I know you feel a little lost a lot of the time, I know there are a lot of things about yourself and about your life that you do not understand right now, but love is not found in a boy who cannot love himself. You cannot find yourself in the same love that you lost yourself in.

Your life is not going to be what you thought it would be. I am writing this letter with a mind softened by the grief, a soul strengthened by the fights, a heart made wise from the fallouts. Do not give up. I have to go now, but know that I am writing this letter from a place of power, happiness, and contentment. I love you. One day, we will meet again, and we will both tell stories of how we made it.

what this love has taught me
is that some of the ones we cherish
with all our hearts
are meant to walk with us only
to a certain point in our life
before they turn
and look to us one last time
and whisper goodbye

so, this is what it feels like
to be broken
when you've lost everything
that defined you

you look in the mirror
and you can't recognize
the person staring back at you

she's tired
her eyes are puffy
from the ghost
of the tears that washed
her happiness from her spirit

she stares in the mirror
and her mind replays
the things she wishes to unsee
the memories that gave her scars
and brought her to her knees

she starts her day with emptiness
and lets life pass her by
the hurt transcends into numbness
and she begins to lose faith
that life will ever
feel genuinely happy again.

~when everything falls apart

✧ THE ✧

HURT

the world stopped turning
the day you left

you might not have felt it
but I did

I felt it

in every crack in my heart

the tears wouldn't stop
and the heaviness consumed
my entire being

when you left

the sun stopped shining
the butterflies hid away

and life as I knew it
drained with the tears
that fell from my cheeks

somewhere in between then and now
the "I love you" text you sent
on a random Tuesday
turned into your last
your face turned into photographs
I memorize so I don't forget your smile
your voice turned into voicemails
replaying every night as I pray to God
that you're okay
your memory turned into promises
I make to become a better me
so that one day I can ensure
that I'll be hugging you again
your favorite shirt turned into
my favorite shirt, a blanket I wear
to remember you

somewhere in between then and now
grief became my best friend
and I lost you completely

I swear I felt the moment when
you took your last breath
grief woke up and needed to find
the closest home, so she found me
she nestled into my heart
shook me awake and whispered
"look up to the sky"

it was like some veil
had been lifted
the clouds parted ways
and the sun shined through
warmth kissed my cheek
and somehow I knew
you were up there
smiling down on me

I feel like I failed you
I have so many things I need to say
so much regret inside of me
half the people I know today
have never met you
they've never seen your smile
they've never heard your laugh
they've never witnessed
how kind and forgiving your heart is
and the worst part about it
is that I'm afraid to say
that I no longer have it in me
to share the happy memories

I wish the world was kinder to you
there was so much you wanted to see
so much I wanted to share with you
now I tell it to you in between silent prayers
and tears before I sleep

I hope you're up there listening

Kayla McCullough

lately it seems like I can't move on
there's now a hole in the world
where you used to be
and somewhere along the way
I think I lost myself in it
I smile when I need to
but deep down I'm gasping for air
choking on the tears
that never seem to end
when will "the old me" return?
I wish for the day when I can smile
and not feel guilty about it
honestly, I think I've started
grieving for myself
isn't that ironic?
you're no longer alive
and neither am I

the last thing you gave us
was an empty house
full of memories
that left us crying on the floor
heartbroken seeing that this
was your life after we left
it's the last thing we have
now that you're gone
and the thought of someone else
another family
making memories and living here
somehow seems wrong
maybe it's best
to just tear it down
rather than let go
of a dream you once had
but this was never your home
these walls never comforted your spirit
and these floorboards never
held you upright
losing this is not like losing you
all over again
but why does it feel the same?

Kayla McCullough

in another universe
it would have been me instead of you

in this universe
I pray to God for it to have been me instead of you

in a heartbeat, without hesitation
I wish it would have been me instead of you

I don't think the part of me
that believes there is a light
at the end of this darkness

has ever met the part of me
that regrets not hugging you tighter
the last time I saw you.

I should introduce them someday.

Another birthday has come and gone
without hearing from you.
My memory replays
the sound of your voice over the phone,
but I think the pitch is off.
I can't see your eyes. Does your smile
reach them? Now that I think about it,
I think your laugh was happier.

I think I'm forgetting you.

every part of me is terrified
I've witnessed a moment
where love wasn't enough
I've cherished something
that death did too

To my daughter on her wedding day:

Don't cry for me, please, and don't be sad.
I've already seen you in your princess dresses,
your crowns, and your jewelry. I've already
danced with you to slow music, and I've been
here all along walking through life with you.
I've seen you fall in and out of love, and I
promise you, this time you got it right.

I promise I've missed nothing, and
I'm here standing by your side.

I've never been a man of many words,
but please always remember,
I loved you first.

And if you save a seat for me, know
that it will not be empty. Every time
you look this way, I will be here,
smiling and dancing with you.

the sky is gray again
rain clouds loom and threaten
to take the peace and happiness
of what was promised

the wind blows and stirs
the fresh dirt of the grave where
I buried the memories of us

it's as if the pain of losing everything
will never fully escape my body

every time it rains
I'm haunted

the gentle pitter-patter against the
cold
hard
dying
earth where you lie
awakens me from the numbness

and the storm outside matches
the storm swelling in my heart
and I succumb to the memories
that I've spent months running from

I showered at your place last night
it wasn't the first time
maybe the fifth or sixth
and I used your hairbrush
I'd forgotten mine at home
little strands of gold hair peaked
out between the bristles
it's beautiful really
how we leave traces, remnants of ourselves
throughout this life
I've always loved your hair
the dark curls soften your features
dark, not golden
a lie hidden in plain sight
I blink back the tears
and suck in my breath
I open the bathroom door
and I feel something I didn't think
I'd ever feel again—
little pieces of my heart break

I've never been in this situation
where one day I'm in love
and the next I realize
that nothing is perfect
and the person I was in love with
has been cheating on me all along

no one talks about what happens
after they forget you
after you see them
moving on with someone else
the pain that comes with
knowing that they're never
coming back

the promises that will remain forgotten
the journal entries that will hold truth
to every waking moment feeling
utterly alone and lost

the pictures that are gaining dust
and fading with time
they hold memories and paint
a thousand words of times
they made you feel
worthy and enough

no one talks about the innocence
that's been stolen
the memories that haunt you
and hunt you down
making it known
and letting you believe
that you've been
forgotten

I wonder if I'll ever stop falling in love with the wrong people or if I'm just destined to always meet the right people at the wrong time. Each love I fall into ends the same way, but it doesn't stop me from believing that this love will be my last. I want so badly to believe that the next time will be different, but no matter how hard I try, I never meet people when they're ready. They're either still hurting from a love that they lost or they've closed their hearts because they're scared. Maybe it's okay that these people are never permanent, because once they leave, I learn a little more about me.

it was painful, loving you
it was painful, leaving you

I know that you're not the one for me
but right now, knowing that doesn't help
because I really wanted you to be
and knowing better
doesn't equate to feeling better

I wanted it to be you so badly
that I stripped away pieces of myself
so that there would be bits of me
scattered throughout your life
in hopes that one day
you'd want it to be me too

my worst fear was once losing you
watching you move on without me
seeing you happy somewhere else

my worst fear is now learning how
to cope and live in a world
you're no longer a part of

this grief of mine feels inescapable
and time will always be
my worst enemy

It's not about the times when you lifted me up with your love. It's about the times when your love placed my heart six feet underground, deeming me unworthy, unappreciated, and undeserving of compassionate, consistent, and intoxicatingly dedicated love.

I was only ever just a beginning to you, a love where you learn everything you don't want from someone. A placeholder to occupy your time until you found the person who you were really looking for. But there was a time where I was the one you ran to, because no one else understood. The one who was always there to listen when the rest of the world would shut you out. You'd come to me so broken, and I'd be there, carefully mending you back together. But before the final piece could be placed, you'd run away. You were always the life of the party, never a homebody, and I was only ever just a beginning to you, never an end.

what if we were both wrong?
that night we said goodbye
what if timing and distance
were just excuses we used
to move on with
our fleeting lives

because I know
you know
that on that night the stars aligned
and the love we shared
the memories we made
were seen across the galaxies

I just wanted you to know
I never wanted to say
goodbye

I will forever be somewhere between
all you ever wanted
and everything you said
you could never love

Kayla McCullough

I sit here for hours
thinking so hard and feeling so little
I wish I could sleep my days away
my dreams are the one place
I get to see you again
I live life through photos
saved in my camera roll
I grasp at the memories painted
across the screen
I live with grief every day
we've become close
so close that I wish
she would leave
and you would come back
I'm tired of living without you

It's midnight again, and you are the only thing on my mind. There are so many things I wish I could tell you, so many things I wanted to tell you, but I lost track of time. It seems time has tricked me into believing that it was infinite. I took it for granted, and now it is the one thing I cannot get back. I'm sorry for believing that it belonged to us. For assuming that I could hold you forever. For thinking that I had more of it. I'm sitting here regretting not telling you how much I missed you while I had the chance. I'd trade any of my tomorrows for a chance to see you, to tell you exactly what you meant to me, and to not live a life full of unspoken words.

Deep down I've always known that you'd leave someday. Sooner or later, the bags would be packed, the closet would be empty, and the side where you slept would be cold. I just never assumed you'd leave so soon.

The different types of sadness come and go like the tides of an ocean; one moment I'm free, and the next, I'm drowning.

Why do you love him so much? my mind asks.

And I don't know what to say; how could I when I never understood why I let you destroy me.
The way you left was like I meant nothing. And all the memories we made never existed to you. But they did to me.

It's been forever, and here I am, wasting my time still lost in them.

come and kiss me one last time
call me and tell me
that you're catching the last flight
tell me you love me
and then kiss me again and again

because I can't and I'm afraid I won't
and I don't know how to say
goodbye to you

so, do something
say something
so that this goodbye
was never our goodbye

When I first started missing you, I realized that maybe I would never stop loving you. It was like my heart was screaming and no one could hear. I felt hopeless. Like nothing in this world could save me. Like nobody would understand the weight of this heartbreak. I felt ashamed. That somebody could be that important to me. And when it was over, and you were gone, I almost wished that I could have all the bad things back so that I could find peace in the good.

But as the days pass, I'm finding that I can go hours without thinking of you. The silence doesn't seem as hopeless, and the emptiness doesn't feel as unforgivable. It's during these moments when the future doesn't seem as foreboding and healing seems possible. I live in these moments.

It's cruel, the way the universe pulls two people together, only to tear them apart. One day you meet someone, and for some unworldly reason you feel like you've known them your entire life. Every sense of déjà vu tumbles down on you, and you just know, without a doubt, that this person is someone special. Perhaps they're an angel sent down to guide us and love us in ways we cannot love ourselves. Whatever the reason, watching them walk away is soul-crushing.

Kayla McCullough

I wish I would have known
which moments were meant to be our last
I would have lived in them a little longer

she sacrificed every moral
to feel the slightest bit of love
she became everyone's version
of the perfect person
while completely draining herself
for others to feel full
she lost herself and her way
she burned herself into ash
in the name of loving someone else

she's the girl
nobody can commit to

I want to be the one you pick
the one you choose out of a crowded room
the one you can't take your eyes off of

I want to be the one you fall deeply
madly in love with
and I want to hear you say it
in between kisses and the words
you're so beautiful and *I do*

I want to be the one who stands by your side
fifty years from now
with gray hair and wrinkled skin
and if our story had to end
I'd have a place by your side up in heaven

but it seems life had different plans
because we broke up in the same place
I imagined this future with you
in the same place we first kissed
where you first told me you loved me

how like me this is

to imagine a story with unspoken
*I love you*s and forever promised goodbyes

I woke up today and my sheets were still covered in tears from the night before. My eyes were red and swollen. My legs were tired, and my head was spinning. And all I wanted was to go home. To hug my mother and tell her how much I love her. To tell her it hurts to be anywhere but here. That the pain is too heavy to carry this time. That the pain is harder to handle this time. That the pain may not go away this time. All I want to do is to go home, but home is where you are, and I don't want to see you. Everything in this town reminds me of you. You ruined this town for me. I doubt if it'll ever feel like home again. So, I'll pack up my bags and I'll stay out. I can go everywhere, but I can't go home.

Grief found me again today, and this time she brought a friend. His name is Guilt, and he is very unkind. He makes me feel regretful for not consuming my days with memories of you. He makes me feel shameful for finding happiness in unexpected places. He fills me with sadness for not stopping by every time I'm in town. Guilt is not a very nice friend; he makes me feel emotions I want to hide from. I've been running from Grief, but it seems as though I cannot run from her for very long. Today she found me in the middle of a sunny street on a beautiful day and brought a friend I could not turn away.

there's this place in my head
where I go to imagine different endings
I hold my breath and count to ten

one two three
imagine a time when we never met

four five six
tears that have traced down my chin

seven eight nine
reasons why you were someone beautiful to me

ten eleven twelve
I was supposed to open my eyes at ten

thirteen fourteen fifteen
I never want to forget you

. . . sixteen seventeen eighteen nineteen twenty . . .

maybe it takes longer than ten seconds
to move on from your *I love you*s

someone is your everything
and then they are nothing
and the world keeps on moving

the beautiful thing about heartbreak
and the world we live in
is that it implores you to be strong
to move on
to not wait for someone
who might never come
to set things free

you might not know
what happens now
or where you'll go
but being honest and true
with yourself
and everyone else
and feeling the things
you wish not to feel
are what help your soul
let go and heal

There are people I've met and wished that I could go back in time and erase the moment when our souls aligned. To save myself from the agonizing heartache that came with loving them. And then there's you. Despite knowing that our story ended way too soon, there's never been a fraction of a second when I'd ever want to forget meeting you.

what I've learned is that timing isn't always synonymous with greater love

lately I've been thinking
that if you'd ever come back
ever want to try
to truly love my heart
I think it might still
wish for goodbye

it'd probably long
for your lips to touch mine
and for your hands
to travel up my spine

but secretly
it'd be yearning
for yours to disappear
like it did last time

because our fire
was born in disaster
and a second chance at love
would be softer

you'd kiss me differently
and you probably wouldn't taste
like whiskey

your hands would be gentler
and they'd probably never be
as full of desire

I'm not sure if I like
love with you a second time
I'm not sure if I like
this new softer love

I want a love
as if nothing
ever happened

though I've been missing you all this time
I wonder what's been crossing your mind
have you thought of me
at least once
since we said goodbye?
because honestly the thought that we
will end up as strangers
after everything we shared
that someday I'll forget
your voice and your smile
and the person you were
haunts me more than anything else

Kayla McCullough

you know the distance
and the timing
and the 2 am calls
never made a difference to me

when you told me
you loved me
for the very first time
I waited and waited
for it to be followed
with why
I love you because . . .
is all I've ever known
three words followed by
an ocean of reasons
somehow leaving you
with an abundance
of questions

but *I love you* alone
is quite different
it's a feeling
that fills every void
in your heart

it's both simple
and complex
so incredibly intricate
and naturally simplistic

a feeling
that leaves me wishing
that all roads would
lead me here
not only to be loved
but also to be known
by the ones
I hold near

Kayla McCullough

nothing hurts as bad
as waiting for someone
you know is never
coming back

Grief and I have been at war for quite some time now. It's like she revels in my undoing. Day after day, week after week, she's there knocking me down, and every time I think she's won, she gives me her hand and stitches me back up. She likes to remind me that I've died while living.

"Why?" I sob. "Why do you return?"

But Grief does not answer me.

Instead, she continues to knock me down and pick me back up. I cried while I was with friends and family. I cried while I was alone in the shower. I cried while I was in the car driving. I cried while I was dreaming. I cried and cried and cried until I couldn't cry anymore.

"Why?" I repeated into the night.

Grief collected me one more time. She opened her arms and became a blanket around my soul and said, "You must feel the hurt to heal. It hurts because it was love. It hurts because it was powerful. It hurts because it was meaningful. Healing comes from the journey you take rediscovering that Love and I are the same."

"Do you think we'll ever see each other again?"
        was the last thing I ever asked him.
"Not this time,"
        he promised.

and it's taken me all these years
to believe him

I wonder if that's why I spend
so much time sheltered
in my imagination

I sincerely hope
that one day you look back
and remember us
simply because
for me
the love that we had
has happened only once

and it will forever
be seared into
my memory

to me we were forever
and forever was not long at all

the worst part about all of this
the part that I can't seem
to wrap my mind around
without feeling like
my heart is being squeezed
to the point that it feels
battered and bruised
is that I can't imagine
my life without you

I don't know how
to go on and act okay
when I know
that there will be a day
when you'll be gone

how do I live
with the memories of you
plastered on these walls?
how do I live alone
in this home that built us both?

I don't know why we get to love others
but I do know that the day you leave
there will be a hole in my heart
that will never heal
a place where you'll get to live on
and always be a part of me

I gave you everything
every piece of me
every secret and every dream
and yet, after all of this,
you still walked away
like I was a mere hiccup
in your story

you sit there looking at me
with innocent eyes
telling me that you're sorry
but you weren't sorry
when I didn't know
and that is more telling
than what will ever
come out of your mouth

Kayla McCullough

I fell asleep in the sun one day
and you came back to me

I don't think you understand
how long I've been waiting
for this
for you

I've been waiting for you too
a voice said

I turned and there you stood
I wanted to tell you
all the beautiful things
that have happened
since you left

but just like last time
I could feel the ending
before it came

like a story that was
almost finished

like a writer leaving
a poem before it's done

and instead I say
we never made it
did we?

my eyes flutter open
the sun is gone
and it's raining once more
I guess unfinished endings
are sore to even those
up in heaven

my dreams have always been of you
but every time I close my eyes
your heart has never been with mine
you've always belonged
to someone else

you've never
ever
been mine

Kayla McCullough

I'm covered in broken promises
and bathed in things
that have been left unsaid
by the people who promised
to never leave

you deserved a kinder goodbye
one that wasn't riddled
with lies and heartache
one that never begged you
to sacrifice your kindness
or change the best parts
of who you are
because all you were looking for
was a love to fall into
and when you found it
all you were met with
was the ground

you deserved a kinder goodbye

Kayla McCullough

the breaking starts slow
one moment you are living
and laughing
and making memories
and then a tiny crack
in your foundation appears

over time it stretches
across the surface
you pray for the feeling
to come back
to feel what was lost

then it's in your voice
the doubt creeps in
and shakes you
awakening the need
to change up your life
at any cost

from your throat
the break travels
deeper into your chest
finding a home
in your heart
the pieces unravel
and the pain seeps
deep within

you suffer in silence
reminisce and picture
it all in your head
just wishing for it all
to come back

last night we said goodbye again
I don't know how many times
goodbye has come out
of our mouths at this point
but if I'm being honest
I could live a thousand lives
hearing goodbye
if goodbye promised
to always feel like this

it'll always be like this with you and me
for reasons we can't comprehend
we'll always end up back
in each other's arms
over and over again
drawn to one another like magnets
except nothing good ever comes
out of us being together
how many times have you hurt me?
how many times have I hurt you?
we're like a case of forbidden fireworks
that should have never been lit
we burn ourselves
again and again
one kiss and the midnight sky
is set ablaze
and our worlds are bathed again
in an impossible luminescent affair

she's changed
you can see it in her face
in the way she laughs
her smile
which once lit up the room
now doesn't reach her eyes
she gave you her heart
and you threw it away

she's changed
because when she needed
you the most
that's what you wanted
her to do

you're a fool for thinking your love
would do no harm
for it was your love
that made her heart forget
what real love truly feels like

and what she needs now
what she longs for
is something that will
help bring her back home
once more
to the love within

Kayla McCullough

it's 2 am
three months
since the last time
I heard your voice
black velvet laced
with honey whiskey
the same as it was
back when forever
meant something

it's 2 am
three months
and the first time
you asked me
how I've been
since goodbye
tears streaming down
my cheeks
it was like hearing
every version of hope
all at once

it's 2 am
three months
and the final time
I say *goodbye*
and lose you
just like the first time

I've learned that you will die over and over again for the rest of my life. I loved you with my entire being, and I will grieve you with my entire soul. I've known and loved you in every lifetime, and something like that never goes away. Breath by breath, life by life, I will never stop loving you.

I get it now. Love and Grief are conjoined; you don't get one without the other. When they leave, all you can do is love them and honor them by living in a world of loving them.

Kayla McCullough

they don't understand
the people we run to for comfort
when the world turns upside down
and we can't see around
the storm that threatens
to engulf our very existence

they watch us cry
and with helpless
vulnerable eyes
they tell us to let it go

it's easy to let go
of something
that seems so broken
from the outside

but that's what they don't understand
the rubble they see
was once a castle
the shattered glass windows
were once stained beauty

it's easy to tell someone
to let it all go
when they can't see
the beauty beneath

All you were looking for was someone who was going to stay. Someone who would support you and encourage you to go after your dreams. Someone who was going to be there during the good times and stand by your side during the bad. And if it had to come down to choosing if they would fight for you, the answer would be undeniably *yes*.

all you were looking for
was someone to love you
like you loved them

I'm not a fool. No, he didn't love me,
at least not in the way I imagined love
with him would feel. He's seen my entire body
naked under the moon and stars, and he says
he could love me. But he's never seen me with
wet hair after a shower, with no makeup on
a Sunday afternoon or asleep on the couch
because I was too exhausted
to make it to the bed. He's never hugged me
while I cried or kissed me on the forehead.
And now that I think about it, he probably doesn't
even know my birthday or my favorite color.
And he's probably never seen the birthmark on my thigh.

No, I guess he didn't love me after all.
He couldn't have. Because to him I'm fuckable,
not lovable. *But God, did I love him.*

which kiss
was our last kiss

which "I love you"
wasn't a lie

please tell me
because lately it feels like
I'm losing my mind

your passion's been mistaken
your guilt's shining through

what a warped sense of love
if this is what love is with you

if this is the end
then I hope you'll
always remember
that I wish and pray
for nothing but
the absolute best
for you

you read these lines
and dream of their face
because it is the only way
you can have them

they call at 2 am
waking you from peace
because it's the only time
they want you

perhaps this was never
the definition of love
if love with them
is never safe

Sometimes I'm not okay, and today is one of those days. It's a day where I look up to the sky and ask the stars above why things are the way they are. Why life knocks some people down and lets others stand tall. Today is a day where I'm not okay—not okay at all. But the thing with me is, you would never know. Today I'm wearing sweats that are big enough to fit two of me, but I always wear sweats that are big enough to engulf my body. I'm complaining about the weather and how I'm tired, but I always complain about dreary days and I'm always tired. I'm making jokes about my pain, about how I always seem to fall short of the things I want, but I always make jokes about my pain, and today is like any other day when I make jokes about not being enough. Today is a day when you don't realize I'm not okay, but I wish you would open your eyes and see it.

as I sit and cry
and tell you why
the teardrops
fall off my cheeks

I see the fear and confusion
seep from your heart
the wonderment
of what happened
to the strong person
you once admired

it breaks me
for you to see me
like this

I feel guilty
projecting my broken heart
onto those who never broke it

but please
I'm begging you
say something
that will help heal it

because what you don't understand
is that when your heart is set on something
it will not beat without it

they keep telling me to be strong
but lately it feels like
I'm barely hanging on
how does one be strong
when life feels like its intent
is to always prove happiness wrong?

it's going to get easier
right?
it has to get easier

I used to dream
about being invisible
that if I could choose
a superpower
that would be it

I made up scenarios
of feeling light
and airy
that life could be easier
if no one could see me

there was no pressure
no predetermination
of who I'd be

but today I feel
the weight of choices
an innocent heart chose
because the thing
I've learned
about being invisible
is that it's the heaviest
thing my soul
has ever known

last night I began to wonder
how people get to where I am right now
broken, shattered
a million pieces on the ground

and I like the idea that sometimes
people have to leave
and hearts have to break
for you to learn
what you truly deserve

but after thinking about it now I'm not so sure
that everything is destined to be
because how can some hearts be
so careless? so reckless?

now I think it's in human nature
to want to break each other
into a million pieces
without mercy

to leave those you love most
to suffer alone

and the reality of love
is that it comes and goes
and accepting that is
nothing less than impossible

after you left, you called it a mistake
but to me a mistake is something
you learn from

something you overcome

not something meant to destroy

sometimes people who are fated to meet
don't ever fall in love
sometimes the love comes unrequited
hand in hand with pain and suffering
and in the end one is left wondering
what could have been
sometimes people meet at the wrong time
and say an early goodbye
and sometimes they don't meet at all

but maybe in another time
a different place
or a prior existence
they were yours
and you never had to mourn
someone who never died
a love that still exists
just not in a world where
your heart lives

They say you must follow your heart. That your heart knows the truth your mind doesn't want to accept and despite knowing the damage it's been through, it will always remain true. That someday your heart will thank you for not giving up on love, even after everything you've been through and everything you've seen and everyone who gave you a reason not to believe. They say someday you'll understand why some people had to leave. But today I am disappointed in my heart and in the love that it gives out freely. I thought that when you were in love—even if that person is gone—it would always be there, staring you in the face, reminding you why you loved them in ways you could not define. But it seems that love isn't always like that, and if you look for grand examples of anything from your heart, it will disappoint you.

Sometimes we don't ever really let go. We don't really move on. We just learn to cope with the pain. Grief is forever. Step by step, and breath by breath, she's always there—becoming a part of who you are. We learn to smile while tears are traveling down our cheeks. We learn to laugh while every broken piece moves within us. We adapt. Learn to survive. Learn to live again. We carry on and hope for a better tomorrow.

You don't visit me in my dreams anymore, and if I'm being honest, your name hurts a little less when my friends mention it. Perhaps this is what moving on feels like. My heart will always house memories of you, but they don't hurt me anymore. I've stopped wondering why I was never enough. I've stopped fearing seeing you in a bar with someone new.

Honestly, life has gotten easier since the tears have dried.

Of course, I'm not sure if it's because I'm actually okay, if the emotional strain has lifted, or if it's that there aren't any more tears left to shed. But they've stopped. And this moment feels right.

So, if this is the end of me missing you, I hope someday peace replaces any loss that occurs in your life.

Just like it did mine.

✧ THE ✧ rescue

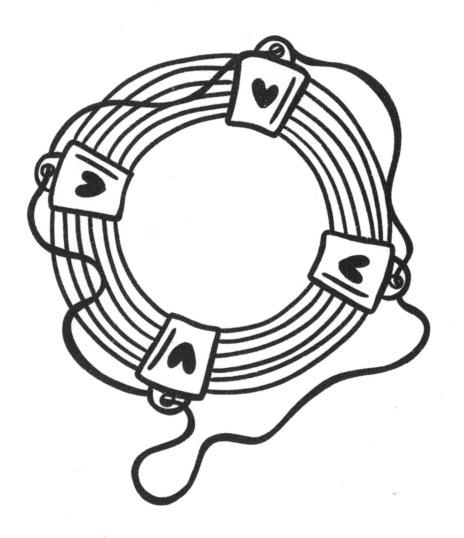

in the middle of your hardest fight
I hear you whispering
that you have nothing left
that you've been forgotten
and your happiness has been stolen
that you feel broken
and helpless

but you are everything

and the emptiness left behind
by those who walked away
is not your undoing
but the space where
you will be rescued
and the home
where you will begin
to build you again

You don't ever have to have a reason to have hope.
You don't have to have evidence, or logic, or any
understanding of what it is. If it's what moves you
forward, gets you to tomorrow, and reminds you
that there is still something worth living for, then it's
something that's worth believing in. Hope is born
between not knowing if it's there and recognizing that
there's so much more to life than what we know.

don't let the heartbreak
convince you that
you're not ready
for the next chapter
without them

it's okay to be unsure
of what's coming

it's okay to cling on to
a little bit of hope
if that is what gets
you through to tomorrow

open the corners of your heart
let the light shine in
and know that you can simultaneously
acknowledge your heartbreak
and begin to love life again

I'm sorry

to the girl who once believed
in fairy tales and romance novels
love rarely comes in the form
of glass slippers and white knights
I'm sorry that hope played
the villain in all of your stories

to the man I fell in love with
before our love was ready
I'm sorry I didn't wait
a few more nights
before those three words escaped
from deep within my heart

to those reading this book
remember that you are
the storyteller of your life
and if you are in love
even with those keen to hide it
never be afraid to live within it

Kayla McCullough

I'm not good at letting things go
I tend to hold on too tightly
to people
to places
to moments lost in time
to everything
I stretch out their happiness
until little holes form
as if life is trying to move on
and let go of you without me

grief found me today
and she had only one wish
for me to love myself
in the same way
you loved me
so, on the days
where I miss you the most
I love myself harder

I know that the goodbye
is long overdue
and still I wait
as long as possible
because I fear being left
with a vacant space
in my heart

you will heal
but it takes time
and every moment spent
will be worth it

the best people aren't happy, they're whole
so, if trees can teach themselves
how to blossom after the winter,
then so can you

you will never understand what changed
why they said the things they did or
how making you feel less than human
was something they were okay with
you can wish to go back to a time when
you were all they ever wanted
or you can accept that this ending
was always meant to happen
and you should let go of what let go of you

they've already let you go
and I know that you can't see that yet
your misguided hope is blinding you
from the reality that's staring at you
but trust me, the empty bed
isn't just because he's out with his friends
the unanswered phone calls
aren't just because he's at work
the fear and doubt you're feeling
aren't just fear and doubt
you've known it for a while
you felt him leave months ago
and the only thing you should do now
is let him let you go

When you begin to doubt, please always remember:

You are too smart to believe the things they say. As soon as you open yourself up to them, they will walk away.

When you begin to feel their hesitation, please always remember:

You are too loving to want to spend your time with someone who won't give you theirs. If they can't spend their days with you, then they'll never spend their life with you.

When you begin to forget, please always remember:

You are too good for people who don't know what love is. Every time they get close to it, they run away. They'll never mend a heart like yours because they're the kind of people who keep breaking them.

what good is their love
when their love
was never good to you

it's not that you haven't let them go
or tried to move on
but that you're still trying to heal
the wounds they caused

the bruises from their lack of empathy
and the scars from their dishonesty
caused trauma that doesn't
just disappear overnight

instead, the stresses
that this relationship brought you
have overflowed into
your present and future life

you haven't moved on
or let them go
because you haven't let go
of the pain they caused you

I love hard, to the point where I can sometimes lose myself in others, and maybe that's why people don't realize that when they hurt me, they do the kind of damage that doesn't just disappear overnight. Little pieces of myself break off—my trust, my confidence, my self-worth—and scatter throughout the people I've loved. Each relationship leaves me with questions of what's real and what's not, what feelings are there, and which ones are romanticized. It's hard to get my footing sometimes, but I still believe in love. I believe in the kind of love that shows up for you. The kind of love that never leaves you wondering about whether it'll last forever, because it just does. And I have faith that one day, I will take some of the love I give to others and give it to myself.

at first, letting them go will feel like betrayal
you'll question everything
you'll wonder if you made the right choice
question if what you had was real or not
you'll probably miss them
and long for some kind of closure
something, anything to help you move on
and deep down you're secretly hoping
that they miss you too
but even if they did
they've already taken too much of you
they've used and misused your love
and honestly, that's all you need to remember
to close that chapter of your life
and start a new one on your own

sometimes the biggest lesson you will ever learn
is when not to forgive mistakes
you've already forgiven in your past
and when to leave the people
who have proven that they'll never change
prioritize your peace
and stop tolerating the way
they've gotten used to treating you

sometimes, for a moment, I think about how it would be
me and you again, lost in love
the unspoken undertone surrounding us
that maybe we were, in fact, always meant to be
I find inspiration in these moments
flowers bloom in the space
where your memory was collecting dust
it's fun to fantasize where life could have led me
if I had stayed and fought for you a little harder
but life has a way of moving you forward
you find light where there was dark
closing this chapter was never a mistake
and these memories are those of
comfort and convenience
not fate and destiny
we will never be that
you were someone special enough to remember
but dishonest enough to let go of

I'm begging you—please don't love people who don't love you back. They will never rescue you the way that you're trying to rescue them. They've pushed you away, countless times, because they don't want the help. They don't want to change. The light you see in them is just a reflection of you.

you deserve to be loved
the right way this time
the world has taken
too much from you
the hurt you've experienced
needs to be released back
into the nothingness
so that this heartache
no longer anchors you
to a ghost life
a memory
an experience
that's long gone

Kayla McCullough

when you've lost all hope
I pray that you take the long way home
watch how the trees sway in the wind
how they embrace, adapt, and grow again
you are the tree that is rooted
your tears nourish your dreams
your losses allow new growth
your doubt fuels the birth of change
joy will find you again
let your arms be branches
that carry others
when their branches become weak
let the love you give
be rich enough to help
other trees blossom and grow
let each season that
slowly takes something away
prepare you for what
the next season is ready to give

I don't have it in me anymore
to love those
who cannot love others

to cheer for people
who will not extend the same hand

to be there for someone
who will only disappoint me

I cannot keep giving myself away
to those who only pretend
to be there for me

I extend my gentleness
only to be met with cruelty

I open my heart
to those who have shut theirs

when will I learn the difference
between those who want the best for me
and those who wish to see me fail

Kayla McCullough

let go
of the relationships
that disappoint you

let go
of the friendships
that make you feel
convenient

let go
of the situations
you lose sleep over

let go
of the decisions
that cause knots
in your stomach

let go
of the people
who make your heart ache
every time they can't
choose you

let go and let life set you free

some things have to end
for others to begin

I'm the type of person you'll never hear from again
and it's not because I didn't love you
it's because of how much I loved you
so, I'll let you let me go
because this part of my life is called peace
and if you're not contributing to it
you're probably not meant to be a part of it

I often find comfort in nostalgia. I make a home in my memories, replay them over and over again, like home videos that nobody has the heart to throw away. But I can never make it to the end. I make it halfway through, and life wakes me up. Like it's protecting me from the plot of the story. Like remembering the end will somehow change my present. But at some point, I guess we all have to wake up and remember that life is still happening. The earth is still spinning, and the past won't protect us from the future. At some point, we have to be here for ourselves and for our hearts in the present. We have to be brave enough to hope that the present and the future will be just as good, if not better, than the old memories we are living in.

even when we are broken
we are beautiful

I hope death feels like Christmas morning when I was nine. I'm home for the weekend, and my bedroom door swings open to reveal my awestruck siblings' faces. They jump and run to hug me, excited for me to be home. Magic fills the air. Time stands still. I want nothing more than to stay in this moment a little longer. But my body's getting tired. I can feel sleep creeping up on me. I jump up on the couch next to my mom and shut my eyes. Hours have come and gone, but I don't notice. Instead, I can feel my mom carrying me to my bedroom. I open my eyes for a moment and whisper, "Thank you for having me."

This grief feels as though its sole purpose is to swallow me whole. I can feel the weight of abandonment crawling through my veins, suffocating me from the joy, light, and hope that there will ever be an end to this misery. I close my eyes and I cry. I cry so hard it feels as though my lungs are filled and they are no longer a part of me. I'm hurting and I'm lost, but in this moment, through deep, ragged breaths, I'm reminded that I'm still alive. My heart is still beating and I'm still holding on. I deserve to be here, in this moment, learning how to live with this ache, how to survive and to let go of the pieces of you with each tear that escapes my heart. Every time it feels as though I cannot breathe, I close my eyes and release a piece of this heartache.

No one knows how many times you've knelt and prayed to God, begging for help. How many silent prayers you have to utter throughout your day just to get by. No one knows, and yet you keep on hoping, you keep on wishing, you keep on praying. So, wherever your journey takes you, I pray that you make it. You are strong, even when your heart is exhausted.

in some parallel universe
I know you tried harder
you held on to me tighter
you showed up to the things
that were important to me
you said, "look, my dear,
I will love you always."

I was thinking of you recently, and even though we haven't spoken in quite some time and things have changed, I hope you're happy. I really do. I hope your dreams and wishes all come true. I hope you find someone who kisses the salt off your wounds and dries the tears from your eyes. I hope they bandage the scars on your knees and bruises on your heart. I hope you find someone who sees you and appreciates everything you are. Someone who is not just another lesson. Someone who stays. But most of all, I hope you become this person for yourself too. I know you were only a chapter in my story, but if you'd ever call and want to catch up, I'm free on most Sundays.

I think it'll take a lifetime for me to fully be okay with the loss of you. One minute you were here living and breathing and being such a light in this world, and the next you were gone. The world lost a beautiful soul, I lost someone I loved, and since then, I think I've felt every emotion under the sun. I continue to lose you in pieces every day. First your mail stopped coming, then your things were taken away, and now your clothes have lost your scent. Gradually, the past keeps collecting you, and I'm afraid that one day, I won't have anything left. My broken heart bleeds over your memories, but I'm learning to embrace it, because even in these moments of loss, it is still your hand that guides me through this dance.

And the thing is I would do it all over again—not to change our ending, but to fall in love with our story one more time. As the days pass, I'm remembering less and less of what actually happened and more of what my heart wanted to. I'd like to get to know the real you, from the beginning, one more time.

Kayla McCullough

the only difference between
then and now
is that I do not cry
when your memory
crosses my mind
instead
I release my grief
with each passing day
and watch as you fly away
like a million fireflies

I'm beginning to realize
that I can heal
and miss you
at the same time

What I've learned is that there is always room to feel the things we do not wish to feel. Even on days when we can't exactly put into words what we're feeling, there is always space to validate those emotions. It's okay to have a lot of feelings. It's okay to feel on purpose and with purpose. The things we struggle to find words for are the things that make us feel alive and connected to this world and the people in it. We are all on the verge of breaking down in some way. So, let those emotions inhabit you for a while; feel what they need you to feel, but don't let them possess you. When it's time for them to go, let them go with grace and courage. Joy, love, happiness, sadness, and grief will all return to you one day. Accept them and let them nourish your soul.

you are safe here
here, you are cared for

even in the midst of
self-loathing and destruction

you are safe here
and you are cared for

Our healing cannot be found in other people. No one can love us so much that we can automatically love ourselves. Yes, there are people who will help us on our journey, but their job is not to love us back together; instead, they help remind us of what love feels like. They help us believe that we are lovable—which is the first step in loving ourselves. Knowing that you are deserving of love is the best gift anyone can ever give you.

as much as you would like it to be,
the call that comes wrapped in apologies
isn't always the lifeboat needed
to save your broken body

Kayla McCullough

I don't look for our pictures anymore
or the songs we used to sing during car rides
I don't search for answers anymore
or hidden meanings in your texts
I may still love you
and you may still exist in my memories
but I've realized that you don't get
to take away my peace
I will let you go with each thing
I no longer chase

moving on was never about not loving them
but accepting that loving them isn't worth the pain

By now, you thought you'd be okay. That you would have healed and their memory wouldn't seem so heavy. It's okay to feel defeated from the sadness that consumes your entire body. There is no one way to grieve. Grief stays with us, and over time, she becomes a part of who we are. We shouldn't fear Grief; instead, we should welcome her into our lives, let her nurture the emptiness within us, because in time, the tears we shed in the memory of the one we once held dear water the garden that is their legacy.

there's no cure for missing someone
you know you'll never see again
there aren't any magic words
to make you feel whole once more
but there is peace in knowing
the love you gave them was real

so even though it hurts right now
I hope someday soon
you can find comfort in knowing
that even a love you knew
for a moment
is a love that will never leave

Kayla McCullough

I'm still trying to understand
if loving unconditionally
is my biggest strength
or my greatest weakness

You are not defined by the number of times you've fallen, and your identity is not found in the people who've disappointed you. You are worth more than the brokenness of your past. You are valued beyond the words of those who wish to tear you down. And most of all, you are deserving of healing and forgiveness—especially for the moments when you lost your way.

Sometimes it takes time to realize just how special someone was in your life. It takes distance to realize what you had and what you lost. And with all this time apart, I can honestly admit that I don't think I'd ever let myself go back to us. Everything is so different now, and for once, I think I might actually be okay without you.

it's another night in the universe
where we never made it
I'm standing in my kitchen
making hot chocolate
finding peace in the songs
that the crickets are singing
when my phone rings
it's you
and just for a second
i think about answering
I want more than anything
to hear your voice again
but I know if I answer that call
my body will start to ache
from the memories that I left behind

not wanting to disturb the sanctuary
that this place has turned into
I flip the phone over
and without looking
I silence the call
in another universe
I probably would have answered it
but in this one
the one where we never made it
I made a promise
no more asking myself
how long it will take
to convince you
that I was worth loving

Kayla McCullough

piece by piece
I let you go

between tear-soaked
*I love you*s
and a million goodbyes

painfully but gradually
you left my life

this time
you must
choose yourself

Kayla McCullough

let them go
and don't look back
because they had enough time
and second chances to change
they saw you on your hands and knees
they heard you beg to try to fix
what was broken between you
you gave them your all
and they couldn't change for you
so, if they're not going to make the effort
do it yourself and walk away
choose your peace over their chaos
close that chapter of your life
and start a new one

I never needed closure from you
what I needed was
permission from myself
to just let things be
I needed to accept the ending
and understand that this time
the ending needed to stay an ending
I needed to find the strength
to seek peace and healing
on my own

the secret to closure
isn't in the apology
from someone else
it isn't in avoiding the pain
or numbing the hurt
but rather in
putting energy into cultivating
joy and peace in your own life

once we begin to value
joy over pain
life becomes easier

Kayla McCullough

I've accepted that
things will never be
how they used to be

I no longer get that feeling
of deep longing
when you kiss me
your fingertips no longer
send shivers up my spine

that day when you broke our love
with your callousness
was the day I started loving you
a little less

you lost me
but is that really
such a bad thing?

my heart broke
so that one day
I could see

I'm not interested in relationships that leave me guessing where I stand. I don't want to play games. I don't want to have to analyze the little things to understand what's on your mind. If what you say rarely matches the way you make me feel, I will let you go, because I deserve clarity. If someone is making me doubt my place in their life, they don't deserve to have me in it.

One of the best feelings is when you finally accept that you deserve better and let go of the people who have proven that they cannot love you right. Because there's peace in trusting that closing that door for good will make room in your life for that *one thing* to come in and change everything. You are worthy of good things, and accepting that helps the beautiful things unfold. Trust in what's coming and let go of everything that pushes you to abandon yourself.

Kayla McCullough

one day you will realize
that you are someone
it would hurt to lose

healing doesn't happen in the past
it happens in the today
and the tomorrow

we can't rewrite history
by reliving a hundred memories
of when they said "I love you"
and meant it

true healing begins
when you invest in your heart
and create a new narrative
precisely where you are today

your heart is tired of the lessons
and you want nothing more than
to love and to be loved
so, when you're finally ready to heal
and let go of the things that
absolutely destroyed you
know that the process begins
with admitting to yourself
how much it hurt
because when you begin
to feel your emotions
instead of minimizing them
you start to release tension and trauma
and where there was once fear
there is now a feeling of safety

on the nights when you doubt
the decisions that you've made
remember that there is a version
of you that lives in a universe
of your past what-ifs
they stayed in that lukewarm relationship
and settled for superficial love
they live in that small town
and smile at the same faces
that talk shit about them
behind their back
they work at the soul-crushing job
and have nightly tear-filled phone calls
with their mom

there's a version of you
that's happy enough
in their life of complacency
they have a nice house
with nice furniture
where they have gatherings
with their nice friends
and every night they kiss
a nice, passionless love goodnight
and drift off to sleep

but if their walls could talk
they'd be breathless
from all the secrets
and dreams they run from

don't focus on what you're leaving behind
what you lost or what you gave up

I know it's hard

you're afraid that you won't be strong enough
to let them go
but letting them come in and out
of your life is only breaking you
in halves even more

you'll never be fully ready to let them go
and it'll be a constant battle between
your mind and your heart

but you were born to love
and to be loved

never forget that

the time you spend trying to be good enough
in somebody else's eyes
is time that you don't get back
so, stop trying to prove your worth
to those who cannot recognize
the effort and love you give

the next time you look in the mirror and feel crazy
about the things that happened to you that hurt
know that you're not crazy and they did hurt
the things that they said that broke your heart
did indeed break your heart
don't try to discredit the trauma
that you and your heart went through

you can wait forever
you can hold on for as long as you can
you can fight with everything that you have in you
but there is no person, job, or city
that you can force to be right for you
if it is not
and the thing is
there is nothing that makes us more insecure
than staying around something that is not right for us
so don't pretend
and say that you'll hold on a little longer
and make excuses
for why things aren't working out
if you know it's not right for you
let it go

you've lost so many things during your journey
and you've been displaced from the grief of love
you feel as though your life is unraveling
from the perpetual struggle of seeking
out the warmth of a sweater that you've outgrown
life looks different to you
or perhaps it's always appeared this way
and you needed to shed some layers in order to see it
you're stuck on thoughts of not knowing
who you miss more, them or yourself
but remember, there is beauty in the fact that
you can grieve these things only because
they were once held so closely to your heart
it's a treasure that they filled you with
light and love and hope
but it's also wonderful to experience
heartache and anguish and despair
because they remind you that you had
something worth losing

the end of this
will never become
the end of you

I used to struggle with the idea that once someone
left my life, I had to let go of the memories I made with
them too. That the songs we built our 13-year friendship
on were something I could no longer love. That the
oversized shirts I slept in, from the boy I loved too
much, had to be thrown away. That my favorite number,
the birthday of someone who passed away, had to be
changed. When people become part of our lives, our
lives are then woven with parts of their legacy. You don't
have to forget the things you found comfort in while they
were a part of your life; you can find comfort in knowing
that even though this chapter has ended, parts of it will
always remain.

love existed in the space before
and it exists in the space after
love still exists here

it's true—the people who hurt us the most
are often the people we loved the most
it's the price you pay for love in this life
but even after everything
all the fights
all the tears
all the heartache
I'd never want to change the story we had
because before the heartache
there was love

I think it's okay to reminisce on some memories
and cry for the apologies that you never received
it's okay to spend some evenings walking
hand in hand with your past
and searching for reasons to heal
it's okay to see lingering shadows
of the things that used to bring you joy
the things that time hasn't faded yet
it's okay to miss them
to miss the things
that brought you happiness
but remember,
some roads are difficult to leave
but destructive to stay on

eventually we all become
someone's version of goodbye
not all stories have happy endings
but there are stories with beautiful
middles and beginnings
and those are worth remembering too

one day, when you least expect it
you'll realize your worth
and nothing will ever cage
your heart again

Trust me—there are people in this world who sparkle with hope during the day and who glow with faith during the night. They make the world feel safe, and they see you for all that you're worth. One day, someone like this will walk into your life, and when they do, hold on to them tight.

I never thought it was possible
to fall in love with something
that represented light
when the days were dark

you came into my life
when my head was spinning
and my body was broken
I was struggling to stay afloat
as the tidal waves of inadequacy
swallowed me like a veil of darkness

and you saved me

when I couldn't save myself
you offered me your hand
and became my beacon of hope

when I deemed myself unworthy
you saved me from myself

Some of our hardest battles we fight alone. They're the battles that push us to accept the things that are truly meant for us and to let go of the things that are not. Accepting that everyone we meet, in some form, is a soulmate and parting with them was never a mistake. Accepting that the failures of the things that were once celebrated within our minds were lessons to push us to accomplish something great. Accepting that the prayers we sent to heaven were never ignored—that sometimes no answer is our closure. Sometimes our hardest battle is finding the magic in the things that were given instead of the things we prayed for. Acceptance, in any form, can be truly heartbreaking and magnificently transformative.

I don't want you to run away
or hide
or pretend
that you are fine
when you are not
I want you to be here
with me
and feel this
to be okay
with the fact
that you're not okay
because it is perfectly okay
not being okay
every day

~I'm okay

Kayla McCullough

before I succumb to sleep every night
I close my eyes and hug 21-year-old me
while she cries for the boys
she'll never be enough for
one granola bar and half a hamburger patty
four flights of stairs and miles later
I hold her body upright
as she fights the hunger
I wipe her tears as she pinches the parts
of her body she wishes would disappear
she wants so badly to be loved
but her friends aren't loyal
and her family doesn't understand
and her mind doesn't know when
to stop critiquing her every move

I whisper inspiration through the wind
that blows through her hair
keep going

This is your one chance at life. So, go out into the world and explore it with your whole heart. Fall head over heels in love and crawl out of it in despair. Find the light where there is dark. Live until your heart is a road map of all it has touched. You belong to an extraordinary life. And more than anything, you deserve a life without limits.

Kayla McCullough

I used to guard my heart
but now I guard my peace
because now I know that
my worth is not found in others
and my peace is worth more
than proving it to them

Then, one day, it just clicks.

The torment from your past lifts, and your pain transcends into peace, as you accept that everything had to happen just as it did for you to flourish into who you are now. You see what you've built from the heartache that tore everything down. The forgiveness you've given yourself has released you from the grips of hell. You hold no bitterness or resentment toward the bearer of this heartache. You wish no ill will or cast revenge on them or yourself. The very storm that shook you to your core was a profound gift that set you free.

I'm not going to thank you for hurting me. I'm not going to act like you're the reason why I've gotten to where I am in life today. I will not give you credit for the person I've become. You don't deserve that. Who I am today is because of me; I was there for me when I needed someone the most. I held my own hand. I hugged myself to sleep. I healed for me. This journey allowed me to see that I may have scars, but they will never define me—your love will never define me.

this part of my life is called not giving up
I will pray and pray for the light to come back
I will have hope and faith that one day
these memories won't seem so heavy
that this grief will escape my body

I know that I will not be able
to escape the difficult days
that I will have to learn
to live through them
but I will remain steadfast in my pursuit
to find happiness once more

if I'm strong enough
to have made it through yesterday
I know that I will make it
through to tomorrow
even the smallest steps lead me
to someplace beautiful

I know now
that I am not alone
even though at times
I may feel lonely
and sometimes convenient
to the relationships
around me

I'm not alone

there's always been a voice
deep inside that's been guiding me

talking to and advising me
throughout my journey

I thought it was just my internal conversation
persuading me that what I'm feeling is valid

but I was wrong

it was you here all along
making sure I make it
to where I belong

I'm not alone, I have you

I used to think pain was temporary. You lose someone, you grieve, and then life goes on. You keep living. I didn't realize Grief could stay with me, five years later. Sometimes, I'll be out with my family, laughing, and I'll think of you, and I'll miss you with my whole heart. It's like Grief made a home within me and became my best friend. She's there, willing me to remember, squeezing my heart, and at the same time, I'm laughing, having the time of my life. It's like I'm witnessing joy while simultaneously living in a world of missing you. And then there are times where Grief is all-consuming. She reaches out, touches my heart, and I'm transported to the past, reliving the pain. I feel my heart break all over again, and I realize that I'll be missing you for the rest of my life. It's been years now, and Grief is the one thing I can count on being here for me. She was born out of the love I had for you. So, I guess, in a way, she's all that I have left of you.

I can't remember who I was
before this heartache
before this nightmare
reduced me to ash

and maybe that's a good thing

life as a broken person
has taught me that
there is strength to vulnerability

every sting of pain
you let yourself feel
is worth it

because when you're broken
the one promise
that will always remain
is that you get to start over

and getting a chance to start over
will be the best thing
to ever happen to you

despite how much we may want it
nothing lasts forever
in the end
we must all choose paths
that are best for our hearts
we must all make sacrifices
that make us bleed

in the end
we must all say goodbye
so that one day
there is a hello
from something greater

Kayla McCullough

if love sustains us
we must do everything we can
to return it and preserve it

The most golden parts of our lives are fleeting. Perhaps fate brings our greatest miracles to teach us that nothing lasts forever, that beautiful things may last for only a moment in time but their brevity doesn't take away their significance.

Kayla McCullough

when it comes time to say goodbye
know that there is always a gift
that will be bestowed upon you
sit quietly, let your heart be heard
and while the teardrops fall from your cheeks
look up to the sky
let the beauty above reassure you
that you are going to be just fine
because even in its sadness
the sky is still gorgeous
beauty still exists in the glow
of the moonlit shadows
and where there is falling light
or hope of tomorrow
there is always a promised rise
of better days and resounding suns

you see, the world will sometimes take away
what you cherish most
but no matter what chapter comes next
know that there will always be
a promise of tomorrow
so be thankful for this love
and the warmth it brought you
because beneath this crippling hurt
there are still many love stories that exist
in this universe

You will have days when you miss them. Days when you're tempted to pick up your phone and call them. To check in and see how they're doing. You'll want to ask if they're happy without you, but you won't, because if the answer is yes, it'll crush you even more. That's the artistry of letting love go. You torture yourself with constantly thinking of the memories made in the middle of May until you decide to give yourself the peace your soul desperately craves. Happiness isn't a destination, and you can't mend what is broken when you expect the person who broke it to be the one to fix it. It's okay to still have love for them. To hope that life treats them well. But when you sit outside under a blanket of stars and start to reminisce on what could have been, I hope you are reminded of the endless possibilities that your life holds.

I hope you believe me when I say that healing doesn't mean that you have to forget the pain. It means that the pain you went through no longer consumes and controls your life. It means that there will be a scar where the open wound used to be, reassuring you that if life were to ever get hard again, one day, you will be able to feel like you again.

Sometimes the right choices don't ever feel right. Sometimes they hurt. Though difficult, every single one of them urges us to find the courage within us to pursue what we need, to find what's best for us, rather than what we think we may want. The pain doesn't mean we made the wrong decision. Sometimes it means we found exactly what we needed all along.

Temporary people will leave permanent footprints on your life.

Kayla McCullough

the worst thing in the world can happen
but tomorrow the sun will rise
you will wake
and eat your breakfast
and drink your coffee
and this heartbreak
won't seem so extraordinary

they say that everything happens for a reason
and this morning I think I might believe them
I replay the footsteps of fate
that brought me to where I am today
every tear, every heartache
has gone unplanned and yet I'm still grateful
for each and every one of them
because even though I feel out of control
and lost in the unknown
there's still a part of me that trusts
that this is all leading me to something bigger
than I could ever plan for
and that brings me peace

It is easy to see the darkness when darkness is all around you. It is easy to lose hope when loneliness consumes you. But it takes the mind of a true believer to have faith and see the light. Faith that there is always love that is being extended to you. Faith in the fact that every ounce of your being is love. Faith that where there is pain and darkness, there is healing and light.

so, you've fallen from perfectionism
and have wandered away from grace
the image others had of you is shattered
you showed your pain and you've let
them see the real mess underneath
the brokenness and the guilt that rejoice
in allowing your mistakes to take control
you've let them see your darkness
and the shadows that house your insecurities
you've let them see your weaknesses
and the temptations that weigh you down

where do you go from here?
in the moments when your realness
shines through
who do you run to?
when it's time to reconstruct
the castle walls that keep people out

welcome home, you can leave
your parade of perfectionism
on the coat rack in the hall
this world isn't for people
who pray to go unnoticed
we all have imperfections and scars
imbalances and complexities
we all feel jealousness and self-pity
we all have skeletons
that live in our closets
and we're all running away
from ghosts of our pasts

you're not alone and you never will be

Kayla McCullough

even when you feel like
you are the world's
most broken person

when you don't ever want
to feel love again

on the days when
all you want is to forget
the damage
and numb the ache

know that even then
you are still enough

I promise, you are going to find the things that make you feel free. Free from heartbreak and stress. Free from disappointment and loneliness. You are going to fall into the deepest love—with life, with another human, with your own heart, with everything the light touches. There is a delicate art to letting go, so for right now, be gentle with yourself. Embrace the people who bring you laughter, warmth, light, and love, and allow yourself to be free— everything else is just noise. You are not alone here. You are not falling behind. Everything comes at exactly the right time. Let it come.

Kayla McCullough

in time
this sunset will look more like a sunrise

in time
the nights won't be as lonely

in time
you will find your way again

Those we lose never fully leave us. Their memory becomes part of who we are, and they live on within us. They live in our hearts and are by our side each step of the way. Carefully watching over us and guiding us to a better life. Making sure we live the life they never got to live. We will always miss them because they are part of who we were and who we are today. We can learn to live in a world without the person we love, and we can learn to be almost okay again. Be proud to walk through this life with a part of them in every single thing you do.

Kayla McCullough

hope will be the very thing
that offers you its wings
it will lift you up
and carry you to tomorrow

You're allowed to miss people who were never good for you. People who never cheered for your wins. People who never showed up. People who are no longer a part of your life. Missing them doesn't take away from the healing that you've done. You're allowed to move on and miss memories that you made with someone you loved once.

Let this grief wrap around you. Feel what it needs you to feel. The sadness and anger and fear are here to help you commemorate the love that was between you. The depth of love that you felt for them is remembered through your grief. The ache will always be there, but the emptiness will fill with your memories. It's a privilege to grieve as much as you are.

If today was hard for you, I hope you remember that today was just one day.

A bad day, or week, or month, or year does not equate to a bad life.

You are doing the best you can, and that is enough. You are enough for the life that's meant to be yours. You are enough for the souls who are meant to love you.

The difficult moments will pass. You made it through this day. You made it through last month. You made it through, and that is perfectly okay. Breath by breath, you let go of the moments that were heavy on your heart and your mind.

So, for today, for right now, close your eyes and allow yourself to be sad. If tears trickle out of the corners of your eyes and down your cheeks, let them. Your life is your life and no one else's. Remind yourself of all the times you didn't think you were ever going to feel better and then you did. Let today pass, and in the meantime, be proud of yourself.

Peace will not exist in a space that the universe is urging you to move on from.

there is more to life
than the life that walked away
from you

There will be people in this world whom you'll never be enough for. Your morals will never be high enough. Your successes will never be celebrated. Your thoughts and opinions will never be heard. And who you are as a person will never be measured by how much you've changed but instead by how they perceive your past. Their dissatisfaction stems from their insecurities, and their cruelty makes them feel powerful. But the weak are cruel, and gentleness can be expected only from the strong. In the end, their judgments truly have nothing to do with you, and accepting that you'll never be enough for them is liberating—for the simple fact that you free yourself from their attempts to control you.

Sometimes it's not the person we miss but who we were
when we were with them.

you think you deserve to be sad
to feel this heaviness every day
but it is not okay
and you do not deserve it

it is difficult to have faith
that this heaviness will lift
but faith is more powerful
than hope; it does not fade
have faith in the love
within yourself
so that one day soon
you will come home
to you again

Sometimes, love can exist more in our heads than in our hearts. We build people up, fall in love with who we think they are, and our world comes crashing down when they show us exactly who they are not. We can fall for someone's potential more easily than we can fall for their reality. Simple thoughts turn into stories. Mere moments that made us smile transform into a lifetime of kisses and *I love you*s. And while we're busy daydreaming of a perfect future and plot to our love story, we forget that sometimes not all stories are meant to last. Some relationships are meant only to be chapters in our life. You deserve someone who genuinely sees in you what you see in them. And even if you don't believe that right now, even if it is hard to fathom, it's out there for you. And you are worthy of it.

a heartbreak so profound
will change your life
you just have to
let it move within you

Kayla McCullough

don't ever wish them hate
wish for them to love better
wish for them to find happiness
wish for them to heal

don't hold room
in your heart for hate
hold on to hope that
people can change

There is power in letting go
a power that brings peace and serenity
to a heart that's been heavy for way too long.

There is power in hope
a power that brings light to a soul
that was once shadowed in darkness.

There is power in faith
a power that brings trust
to a heart that's been guarded.

If the love that you have between you doesn't bring you peace, then it's not worth fighting for. If you're not sure if they'd go to the end of the world for you, then they're not the one. If the relationship doesn't allow a safe place for both of you to grow—together or separately—then you deserve better.

the moment you know
that you have to
let it go
is the moment it starts
ruining your peace

and that is a price
your heart never
agreed to pay

Kayla McCullough

As you're reading this, you're probably still thinking of how someone you loved with your whole being could break you in halves and walk away like it was nothing. You're probably feeling like you could never love like this again. That this world is no place for a heart like yours. And you're probably right.

You'll never love like this again; you'll never find someone who loves with just as much heart as you. And this world is no place for a soul like yours.

So, when the world feels heavy and this heartache feels like it's too much weight to bear, know that you will not be whole again in the hands of those who broke you. You cannot feel safe and secure in thoughts that make you feel like you have lost every chance of being happy. There's no one in this world who can love you more than you.

Time will help ease the pain, but it will not heal your broken heart. Eventually life catches up to all of us, no matter what cycle we're in. As you run from your problems, your problems become heavier. As you fight your intuition, your intuition becomes a beacon of anxiety. And although this heartbreak seems as though its sole purpose is to tear you apart, know that your breakthrough is not meant to break you. Life always has your best interest at heart. There is a great plan beyond all of your struggles.

If you feel like you cannot move on from whatever is troubling your heart, remember this:

You have the strength to save yourself. You have the strength to pull yourself out of this darkness, to pick yourself up, even if you are still hurting. You have the strength to heal, all on your own. You have the strength to love your brokenness, even when it feels impossible. Please don't ever forget—you don't need others to save you, you don't need to place your heart in another person's hand for it to be safe, you can rescue yourself. It's always been a strength within your heart.

it is okay to be alone
to not be anything to anyone
because peace is found
in knowing that you are
everything to yourself

Losing yourself is one of the most important things that will ever happen to you. When you feel disconnected to who you are, you give yourself another opportunity to connect deeper to your spirit. Losing yourself, falling off the tracks, and getting curious about life are some of the most pivotal things that will ever happen to you. Embrace the chance that life is giving you to change.

Life has a funny way of making sure we stay on track. Even the things we wanted and never got still pushed us to be right where we were supposed to be all along. Our moments of magic, and those of tragedy, were always intended to keep us on the right track. Life always shows us that even though something didn't work out the way we had planned, it still worked out how it was meant to in the end.

Stop letting other people change the way you see yourself. Your self-worth has never been found in someone else, and their inability to see it does not deem you unworthy. There will always be people who don't want to believe in you. People who think you will never be good enough for your dreams or whatever you're doing. People who exist only to criticize your every move. You have so much to offer this world. You can't spend your whole life proving your worth to the people who don't want to see it, because they will always be blind to your kindness.

You will never be the same again, and maybe that's the point. Maybe you're not supposed to go back to the person you were before this heartache. How you adjusted to life with grief has not only made you stronger but also expanded who you are. You no longer take life for granted, you love as though you will never love again, and you value the people and things you have in your life right now. You're a new person, with a heart full of stories and scars, each guiding you, but never defining you.

I don't think I'll ever stop missing you, and I don't
want to. I'm afraid that the memories I have of you will
disappear. That one day, I won't remember the shade
of brown in your eyes, the way you smiled, or the sound
of your voice. I don't want to forget anything, and that
makes letting you go so damn hard. So, for now, until
there's a day when I can see you again, I will hold on to
these memories. I will remember every birthday, every
Christmas, every Thanksgiving, every Easter, and every
weekend. I will cry when I need to cry, and I will celebrate
your life, because someone as beautiful and as special as
you deserves to be remembered.

One day, this hurt will be behind you. What you thought you'd never be able to move on from will be a lesson you get to look back on. The mountains of anxiety and helplessness that consumed your mind will be things you think of for the very last time. The feelings of being lost and alone will be troubles that eventually fade altogether. One day, you will pass this season of growth, and the person you learn to become, to make it to the other side, that person will stay with you forever.

Kayla McCullough

no matter how bad
things are right now
hope still exists
and things will
eventually get better

even if you never see them again
know that the way they held your heart
the way they protected you from the hurt
was their way of loving you
sometimes our guardian angels
aren't just those who live up above
sometimes they're the beautiful souls
who walk beside us

love
like most things
in this world
exists only
if you will it
to exist

You don't need to worry about love. It is everywhere. It is all around you. It is in you. Every day and in every moment, love is with us. It meets us at our best and reaches out a hand at our worst. That's the thing with love—sometimes you carry it, and other times it carries you.

you have not lost them forever
I promise you will start to see them again
in the most unexpected places

they will come to you in the orange
while the sun is rising above the earth
they will reach out a hand and
gently take yours

you will see them in the things
they loved most and
in the people they left behind

I know this grief is hard
but I promise, you will never
have to look far
close your eyes and feel
the strength deep within your heart
and know that a piece of theirs
is in there guiding you

you've had less and you've laughed until you cried
you've had less and rainbows were seen after storms
you've had less and the sun rose the next morning

you've had less and you've fallen in love
you've had less and you were surrounded by people
who loved you
you've had less and you were still enough to them

what will it take for you to be enough for you?

You've always been capable of love. In fact, it's one of your greatest qualities. It's beautiful, the way you show up in this world, unguarded and willing to love those who've hurt you, time and time again—despite all of the ways they've tried to defeat you. There is a resounding level of bravery in how you believe in love and how you continue to love, even when it hurts. Don't let this heartache convince you to harden your heart.

This journey is your own. This grief is your own. This healing is your own.

There will be times when you will break down, when you will be a mess, when you will cry and look up to the sky and ask the heavens above why losing what you loved most was necessary. But the loss of something you loved with your whole heart is never reasonably answered. So, making your way up and over this mountain of grief won't be either.

But you will overcome this.

You have overcome every single heart-wrenching and unexpected thing.

So, let yourself cry. Let yourself break down. Grief is messy and unkind, but you have always had the strength within your spirit to make it through things that break you. And no matter what tomorrow may bring, you will continue to carry that power within you.

The day will come when you look in the mirror and know that you've finally witnessed the other side of this heartbreak. Your survival and triumph will embolden you to love bigger and better. Your scars, from the painful journey across the bridge where you both ripped and repaired parts of yourself, will show proof of your willingness to love others and how you've come to love yourself.

The other side of this heartbreak is an incredible place to see the powerful weight of your story.

If you have been given a chance to change, I hope you take it. If you have been given a chance to grow, I hope you lean toward the light. If you have been given a chance to learn, I hope you gain all the wisdom you can. This world does not test us by chance. Everything that happens aids us in uncovering the truth of who we are— our only purpose is to find who that person is and learn to trust them.

Your walk with Grief will be the saddest and loneliest journey that you will ever take. There is no right or wrong way to do it. The only way around it is through it, and the worst part is that the journey never ends. Grief stays with you; she grows with you. You hold on to the pain because it's the only thing that makes you feel connected to the people you've lost. This journey is a messy and awful place to be. Grief is an unfixable weight that you will carry on your back, but she is also simply an extension of love.

You may think that the worst type of crying is the kind that people see—the breaking down in the grocery store or the wailing on street corners. But it isn't. The worst type is the kind that hides away in your soul. Years may come and go, but your soul continues to weep. It gasps for air that never comes. Exhausted from the endless fight, a part of it withers and dies. And though you might think it wise to throw out the piece of you that died, instead allow it to create a scar on the part of you that is still living. Your soul may never heal from the weight of this grief, but the experiences it collects along its journey allow you to create a safe space to remember the people you've loved.

Kayla McCullough

life will be beautiful again
no matter what's shifting
or what revelations are happening
everything in life comes full circle

you end where you begin
you love to hurt
then you hurt to love
you let go of what you care for
so that it can find its own way

life is full circle
love is full circle
heartbreak and loss are full circle

some of the world's
most beautiful things
break us
so that one day
they can renew us

you lose people in your life
when you never expect to lose them
you meet people in your life
when you never expect to meet them

God has a funny way
of showing you lessons
of teaching you the painful reality
of love and timing

strangers will turn into friends
friends will turn into lovers
and lovers will turn into strangers
once more

it is promised that people
strangers, family, friends, lovers
will walk in and out of your life
never knowing who will change it

there are times when
love will come and take you by the hand
and others when you will be greeted by heartbreak

everything happens right when it's supposed to
little things become big things over time
our only job is to step out of the way and let them

This journey has always been between you and you. It was about how you learned to stop giving all your love out and to reserve some for yourself. It was about how you walked a path full of loneliness and despair and learned what you needed to let go of to make the journey less heavy. It was about how you learned to see yourself with more love and tenderness and others without rose-colored glasses. It was never about finding someone else to make you feel whole when you were broken. It was always about you and you. You made you whole again. This story was always about how you opened your heart to yourself.

You begin with nothing and end with everything.

~healing

Dear Reader,

When I began writing *Glass Hearts & Unspoken Goodbyes*, I was lost in every area of my life. My days were consumed with self-loathing and destruction. I didn't understand the beauty behind saying goodbye and how grief emulates the love you have for someone when they leave. I was heartbroken and stuck.

As I wrote, all my emotions spilled out: the ones I pushed away, the ones I was too scared to feel, the ones that ended up saving me from my worst fear and the worst heartbreak I had ever experienced.

One of my most difficult realities, and the one thing I fear most, is that one day the hearts I love will no longer walk beside me. Through writing *Glass Hearts & Unspoken Goodbyes*, I found peace in their goodbyes. I learned that grief is a journey of reorienting the heart and accepting that it will forever be a part of you.

Thank you for allowing me to share my story with you. I hope that somewhere in this book you discover new depths of love. May it remind you that love is not to be feared, it is to be preserved and lived within.

Kayla

acknowledgments

Following your dreams is never easy. It takes passion, dedication, and heart to weather the storms that try to knock you down. Mom, you've never failed to inspire me or to guide me. You've always been there to pick me back up, and I will never be able to thank you enough.

To my siblings and my dad, thank you for always being a listening ear and a helping hand. You never fail to show up when I need you. I will forever be grateful for everything you've done.

And lastly, to my loving partner, Turner, and my amazing team at Andrews McMeel Publishing, Kirsty Melville and Danys Mares, thank you for believing in me and helping me bring this amazing book to life. It's an honor to have such inspiring and uplifting people be a part of this journey.